KT-484-965

Rick Stein
FISH
TEN RECIPES

WEIDENFELD & NICOLSON

Rick Stein and his wife Jill opened The Seafood Restaurant at Padstow, Cornwall, in 1975, as a small, harbourside bistro selling locally caught fresh fish. It has become one of the best-known restaurants in the UK, with an international reputation, drawing customers from as far as Australia, Japan and the United States. It has won awards from all the major food guides, and was named Restaurant of the Year by *Decanter* magazine in 1989 and by Egon Ronay in 1996 and Seafood Restaurant of the Year by *Hotel and Restaurant Magazine* in 1998, 1999 and 2000.

Rick Stein's first cookery book, *English Seafood Cookery*, was the Glenfiddich Food Book of the Year in 1989. He has written four more popular cookbooks. He writes the occasional piece for several national newspapers, among them *The Sunday Times* and the *Independent*.

Rick Stein's first BBC-TV series, Taste of the Sea, was one of 1995's most successful television cookery programmes. It won the Glenfiddich Television Programme of the Year Award. It was accompanied by a book of the same name, which was chosen as the André Simon Food Book of 1996. His second BBC-TV series, Fruits of the Sea, was shown in 1997 and was even more popular than the first. In 2001 he won the Glenfiddich Television Programme of the Year Award for The Seafood Lover's Guide and the Glenfiddich Trophy for his lifetime contribution to food and drink.

CONTENTS

Cooking fish I am always looking for subtle combinations of flavours; if this can be achieved with the least possible ingredients then so much the better. I am also a believer in respecting the texture of the fresh fish. With these tenets in mind, I have collected ten of my favourite recipes, some first courses, some main courses, and several to serve either purpose.

The recipes cover a variety of cooking methods, including poaching, which is an excellent way to cook oily fish like mackerel, herring, trout and sardines. Quite a lot of oil is released into the water, leaving firm, well-flavoured fish.

Another favourite is cacciucco, a marvellous Italian fish stew, although I feel rather self-conscious about producing my own version of a dish which brings with it the same sort of arguments about the correct recipe as does bouillabaisse. Some recipes include the ink from squid and cuttlefish, some don't. I think it's a good idea to use a certain amount: with the tomato it gives the stew a beautiful reddish-brown colour. Use a mixture of three or four types of white fish; avoid oily fish.

I hope these are the sort of fish dishes you are going to love and will want to cook often.

Rick Stein

'**Reach not** after morality and righteousness, my friends; watch vigilantly your stomach,and diet it with care and judgement. Then virtue and contentment will come and reign within your heart, unsought by any effort of your own; and you will be a good citizen, a loving husband, and a tender father – a noble, pious man. Before our supper, Harris and George and I were quarrelsome and snappy and ill-tempered; after our supper, we sat and beamed on one another, and we beamed upon the dog, too.'

Jerome K Jerome, Three Men in a Boat

RECIPES

Serves 4

400 g/14 oz fresh salmon fillet, skinned
125 g/4 oz smoked salmon
1 large garlic clove, very finely chopped
3 shallots, very finely chopped
1 tablespoon fresh lemon juice
$^{1}/_{2}$ teaspoon salt
12 turns of the black pepper mill
pinch of cayenne pepper
few drops of worcestershire sauce

To Garnish

24–32 sprigs of lambs' lettuce
extra virgin olive oil
balsamic vinegar
coarse sea salt
coarsely ground black pepper

SALMON TARTARE

Cut the salmon fillet and smoked salmon into very small dice. Place in a bowl, add the remaining ingredients and mix well. Line four 8 cm/3 inch ramekins or similar containers with clingfilm, leaving the edges overhanging. Divide the salmon mixture between the ramekins and press down lightly, so that the tops are smooth. Now invert the ramekins into the centre of four large dinner plates – the bigger the better. Remove the ramekins and the clingfilm.

Arrange 6–8 sprigs of lambs' lettuce around the edge of each plate. Drizzle the rest of the plate, and the leaves, with a little olive oil, add a few drops of balsamic vinegar in between the streaks of oil, and then sprinkle with a little sea salt and black pepper. Serve at once, with a bowl of extra salad if you wish.

Serves 4

- 2.3 litres/4 pints mussels
- 1 tablespoon Thai fish sauce
- juice of 1 lime
- 1 garlic clove, finely chopped
- 1 fresh red chilli, seeded and finely chopped
- 2 teaspoons finely chopped fresh ginger
- 2 tablespoons sesame oil
- 1 bunch of spring onions, thinly sliced
- 2 tablespoons roughly chopped fresh coriander

MUSSELS WITH CORIANDER, CHILLI, GARLIC AND GINGER

Clean the mussels (page 35) and place in a large saucepan with the fish sauce, lime juice, garlic, chilli, ginger and sesame oil. Cover and cook over a high heat for 3 minutes or until the mussels have opened.

Scatter over the sliced spring onions and chopped coriander and turn everything over in the pan. Serve at once.

Serves 4
325 g/12 oz white fish fillets (lemon sole, whiting, pollack), skinned and boned
50 g/2 oz fresh crab meat
4 scallops, with the corals
1 egg white
salt and freshly ground black pepper
150 ml/ 1/4 pint double cream, chilled
pinch of cayenne pepper
1 tablespoon roughly chopped fresh chervil
a little sunflower oil

To serve

Chambéry and sorrel sauce (page 36)

GRILLED FISH SAUSAGES WITH CHAMBERY AND SORREL SAUCE

Cut the fish into small pieces, place in a food processor and chill for 30 minutes. Cut the crab meat, scallops and corals into 1 cm/½ inch pieces and chill. After 30 minutes, add the egg white and seasoning to the fish and process until smooth. With the machine running, pour in the cream in a steady stream, making sure that you complete this stage within 10 seconds (if over-processed, it may curdle). Season the crab mixture with salt, pepper and cayenne, then fold into the fish with the chervil.

Divide the mixture into eight and spoon on to eight pieces of clingfilm, placing the mixture slightly to one side. Form into sausage shapes, about 12 cm/5 inches long, then carefully roll up in the clingfilm, twisting the ends firmly to seal. Fill a large, deep frying pan with water and bring to a gentle simmer. Reduce the heat and poach the sausages for 8 minutes. Transfer the sausages to a bowl of cold water for 2 minutes. Lift them out of the water, remove the clingfilm and brush each sausage with a little oil.

Grill the sausages under a medium heat for 8 minutes, turning occasionally, until golden.

Serve with a little of the Chambéry and sorrel sauce.

Serves 4

2 courgettes
salt and freshly ground black pepper
225 g/8 oz dried linguine pasta
2 tablespoons extra virgin olive oil
175 g/6 oz cooked peeled prawns, thawed if frozen
1 tablespoon chopped fresh dill

LINGUINE WITH PRAWNS, DILL AND COURGETTES

Trim the ends of the courgettes, then cut across the courgettes to make 4 cm/½ inch pieces; cut each piece lengthways into 3 mm/⅛ inch thick slices, then cut each slice lengthways into 3 mm/⅛ inch batons.

Place 1.7 litres/3 pints water in a large saucepan, add 3 teaspoons salt and bring to the boil. Add the pasta, bring back to the boil and boil for 10 minutes or until al dente – just tender but still slightly firm to the bite.

When the pasta is almost ready, warm the olive oil in a small saucepan over a low heat. Add the courgettes and cook gently for 1 minute, but don't let them fry. Add the prawns and heat through for about 30 seconds, then add the dill and season to taste. Drain the pasta, tip into a large bowl and add the prawn mixture. Toss together and serve at once.

Serves 5

900 g/2 lb chilled puff pastry
a little flour
325 g/12 oz skinned undyed smoked haddock
175 g/6 oz cleaned leeks
275 g/10 oz peeled potatoes, boiled
4 tablespoons clotted cream
1 teaspoon salt
10 turns of the black pepper mill
1 egg, beaten

SMOKED HADDOCK PASTIES WITH LEEKS AND CLOTTED CREAM

Cut the pastry into six equal pieces. On a lightly floured surface, roll out each piece to about 20 cm/8 inches square, then cut out six 19 cm/7½ inch circles.

Preheat the oven to 200°C/ 400°F/Gas Mark 6.

Cut the smoked haddock into 2.5 cm/1 inch pieces. Slice the leeks and cut the potatoes into 1 cm/½ inch cubes. Mix together the haddock, leeks, potatoes, clotted cream, salt and pepper.

Divide the fish mixture between the circles of pastry. Moisten one half of each pastry edge with a little beaten egg, bring both edges together over the top of the filling and pinch together well to seal. Crimp the edge of each pasty decoratively between the fingers, transfer to a lightly greased baking sheet and brush all over with more beaten egg. Bake for 35 minutes. Serve hot or cold.

Serves 4
225 g/8 oz unsalted butter
2 fennel bulbs, trimmed and sliced into arc-shaped pieces
1 onion, chopped
1 garlic clove, chopped
300 ml/ 1/2 pint fish or light chicken stock
2 tablespoons dry white wine
1 teaspoon salt
10 turns of the black pepper mill
1 bunch fennel herb
4 hake steaks, about 225 g/8 oz each
2 tablespoons Pernod or Ricard
2 teaspoons fresh lemon juice
2 egg yolks

BAKED HAKE WITH A HOT FENNEL AND BUTTER SAUCE

Preheat the oven to 200°C/400°F/ Gas Mark 6. Melt 25 g/1 oz of the butter in a shallow flameproof dish. Add the fennel, onion and garlic and fry for about 5 minutes or until the vegetables are soft but not browned. Add the stock, wine, salt and pepper and simmer gently for 15 minutes.

Set aside four sprigs of the fennel herb for the garnish. Remove any large stalks and roughly chop the remainder. Season the hake on both sides, lay it on top of the fennel and onion mixture and bake in the oven for 15–20 minutes. Transfer the hake to a warmed plate and keep hot. Remove a quarter of the fennel and place in a liquidizer with the Pernod or Ricard, lemon juice and egg yolks. Melt the remaining butter in a saucepan. When it begins to bubble, turn on the liquidizer and blend the contents for 1 minute. Then slowly pour in the hot butter. Pour the sauce into a bowl, stir in the chopped fennel herb and season to taste.

To serve, spoon the remaining baked fennel mixture on to four warmed plates. Rest the hake steaks partly on the fennel and spoon over some butter sauce. Garnish with the reserved fennel sprigs.

Serves 4
1 tablespoon salt
4 mackerel, about 175 g/6 oz each, filleted

Sauce
225 g/8 oz unsalted butter
2 egg yolks
1 teaspoon lemon juice
a good pinch of cayenne pepper
10 turns of the black pepper mill
1/2 teaspoon salt
2 tablespoons sherry vinegar
1 shallot, very finely chopped
1 tablespoon chopped fresh mint

To garnish
sprigs of mint

POACHED MACKEREL FILLETS WITH MINT, SHERRY VINEGAR AND BUTTER SAUCE

For the sauce, clarify the butter by melting it slowly in a small saucepan until the solids have fallen to the bottom of the pan. Carefully pour off the clear butter and reserve. Discard the solids.

Half fill a saucepan with water and bring to the boil. Reduce to a simmer and rest a bowl over the pan. Add the egg yolks and 2 tablespoons water and whisk until voluminous and fluffy. Remove the bowl from the heat and gradually whisk in the clarified butter, building up an emulsion as if making mayonnaise. Add the lemon juice, peppers and salt.

Put the sherry vinegar and shallot in a small saucepan, bring to the boil and boil until reduced to 1 teaspoon. Stir into the butter sauce, and add the chopped mint. Keep warm in a bowl of warm water.

Bring 600 ml/1 pint water and 1 tablespoon salt to the boil in a large frying pan. Reduce to a simmer, and poach the mackerel fillets for 3 minutes, turning them after 1½ minutes. Lift out with a slotted fish slice and serve on warmed plates, adding the sauce. Garnish with mint sprigs.

Serves 4
4 small sea bass, 400–450 g/14 oz - 1 lb each, cleaned and scaled
2 tablespoons olive oil
coarse sea salt and freshly ground black pepper

Salsa
1 red pepper
1 tablespoon extra virgin olive oil
2 tomatoes, skinned and seeded
1/2 red onion, peeled
2 fresh red chillies, seeded and finely chopped
1 large garlic clove, very finely chopped
2 tablespoons chopped fresh purple basil
1 tablespoon fresh lemon juice

CHARGRILLED SEA BASS WITH ROASTED RED PEPPER, TOMATO AND BASIL SALSA

Preheat the oven to 220°C/425°F/ Gas Mark 7.

For the salsa, rub the outside of the pepper with a little of the olive oil and roast for 15–20 minutes or until soft and slightly blackened. Place in a plastic bag, seal tightly and leave to cool. The skin should come off easily. Cut the pepper in half and discard the seeds. Cut the red pepper flesh, tomatoes and onion into 1 cm/½ inch pieces. Place in a bowl and mix in the chillies, garlic, basil, lemon juice, the remaining olive oil, and salt and pepper to taste. Set aside while you cook the fish.

Make three diagonal slashes in both sides of each fish, then brush with olive oil and season with sea salt and black pepper. Brush a ridged cast-iron griddle with a little oil, place over a high heat and leave until very hot. Add the fish and cook for 4½–5 minutes on each side. Alternatively, preheat a grill to very hot and cook the fish on an oiled grill pan. Serve hot, with the salsa.

Serves 4
1 loaf of slightly stale black olive ciabatta bread
50 g/2 oz plain flour
2 large eggs, beaten
vegetable oil for deep-frying
12 lemon sole fillets, about 65 g/2½ oz each, skinned
lemon wedges, for garnish

Salsa verde mayonnaise
3 tablespoons chopped fresh parsley
1 tablespoon chopped fresh mint
3 tablespoons capers
6 anchovy fillets
1 garlic clove, crushed
1 teaspoon dijon mustard
1 tablespoon fresh lemon juice
½ teaspoon salt
6 tablespoons mayonnaise (page 37)

FILLETS OF LEMON SOLE
WITH SALSA VERDE MAYONNAISE

For the salsa verde mayonnaise, put the first seven ingredients into a pestle and mortar or food processor and grind to a coarse paste. Stir into the mayonnaise, adding more salt if required, and set aside.

Break the bread into small pieces. Place in a food processor and process into crumbs – they do not need to be too fine – then turn out on to a large plate. Spoon the flour on to another plate and pour the beaten eggs into a shallow dish.

Heat the oil for deep-frying to 190°C/375°F or until a cube of bread browns in 30 seconds. Preheat the oven to 150°C/300°F/ Gas Mark 3. Line a large baking sheet with paper towels.

Season the lemon sole fillets with a little salt and pepper. Dip the fillets into the flour, then into the beaten egg and then the bread-crumbs, pressing them on well to give an even coating.

Deep-fry, two pieces at a time, for 2 minutes or until crisp and golden. Remove to the baking sheet and keep hot in the oven while you cook the rest. Serve at once, with the salsa verde mayonnaise and lemon wedges.

Serves 8-10

1 loaf of ciabatta bread
150 ml/5 fl oz olive oil
5 garlic cloves
3.2 kg/7 lb white fish (John Dory, gurnard, cod), filleted
1 cooked lobster
450 g/1 lb squid, cleaned (page 36)
1 large onion, chopped
1 large carrot, finely chopped
2 sticks of celery, finely chopped
300 ml/10 fl oz red wine
400 g/14 oz canned tomatoes
2 bay leaves
2–3 fresh red chillies, slit open
6 fresh sage leaves
900 g/2 lb mussels, cleaned and opened (page 35)

CACCIUCCO

Preheat the oven to 200°C/400°F/ Gas Mark 6. Cut the ciabatta into 1 cm/½ inch thick slices, place on a baking sheet and drizzle with about 2 tablespoons olive oil. Bake for 20 minutes or until crisp. Rub a halved garlic clove over the bread.

Cut the fish into 4 cm/1½ inch thick slices. Remove the meat from the lobster and reserve the shell. Slice the squid into rings.

Heat half of the remaining oil in a large saucepan. Fry the onion, carrot and celery for 7–8 minutes, until beginning to brown. Add the wine, lobster shell, tomatoes, bay leaves, chillies, water and, if you have one, a squid ink sac mashed with a little water. Simmer for 45 minutes. Strain the liquid into another large pan, pressing with a ladle to extract as much flavour and liquid as possible.

Slice the remaining garlic. Heat the remaining oil in the cleaned pan and fry the sage and garlic for 1 minute. Add the squid and fry for 2 minutes, then remove and keep warm. Add the stock and fish, bring to the boil and simmer for 2 minutes. Add the lobster meat, the squid, the mussels and their strained cooking liquid and simmer for 1 minute.

To serve, lay two slices of the crisp bread in the bottom of each plate and ladle the soup on top.

THE BASICS

A NOTE ON CHOOSING FRESH FISH

The eyes should be bright with no red flushes, the skin should be bright, the gills should be a fresh pink or red, not brown. The smell should be welcoming, not fishy. If choosing fillets they should be white, not yellowing. Use the freshest-looking fish on the slab as a yardstick to judge the others.

Ask your fishmonger to prepare the fish for you for the recipes in the book, but remember to ask for the bones to make a good, simple fish stock. It is particularly worthwhile asking the fishmonger to scale the fish, since scales tend to fly all over the kitchen. However, you will need to check that all the scales have been removed, by scraping from the tail to the head with a blunt knife, holding the fish under running cold water.

CLEANING MUSSELS AND CLAMS

Wash the mussels in plenty of cold water and discard any that are open and show no signs of closing again when tapped. Scrape off any barnacles with a knife and pull out the beards. Clams do not have beards, but the shells should be thoroughly scrubbed to remove all sand and mud.

To open, place in a large saucepan with a splash of water or wine, cover and cook over a high heat for about 3 minutes, shaking the pan occasionally until the shells have opened. Discard any that remain closed. Strain the cooking liquid through a muslin-lined sieve and reserve.

PREPARING SQUID

Gently pull the head away from the body – the intestines will come away from the head, which is joined to the tentacles. Reach into the body and pull out the rest of the insides: the plastic-like quill, possibly some soft white roe and an ink sac. Reserve the sac and discard the rest. Detach the fins; pull off the purple skin from the body and fins. Wash out the body with cold water. Slice off the tentacles; discard the rest of the head.

CHAMBERY AND SORREL SAUCE

300 ml/½ pint fish stock (page 37)
75 ml/3 fl oz double cream
2 tablespoons chambéry dry vermouth
15 g/½ oz fresh sorrel leaves
40 g/1½ oz unsalted butter
1 teaspoon fresh lemon juice
salt

Place the fish stock, half the cream and the vermouth in a saucepan. Bring to the boil and boil rapidly until reduced to about 100 ml/3½ fl oz. Meanwhile, wash and remove the stalks from the sorrel, then slice the leaves very thinly.

Just before serving, add the remaining cream, butter and lemon juice to the reduced sauce and boil for about 1 minute, to reduce a little more. Stir in the shredded sorrel and serve at once.

This sauce – based on a simple cream, fish stock and wine reduction – is one I make for various fish dishes.

FISH STOCK

1 kg/2¼ lb fish bones – not from oily fish
1 onion, chopped
1 stick of celery, chopped
2 small carrots, chopped
25 g/1 oz button mushrooms, sliced
1 teaspoon chopped fresh thyme

Place the fish bones in a large saucepan with 2.3 litres/4 pints of water, bring to the boil and simmer very gently for 20 minutes. Strain through a muslin-lined sieve into a clean pan, add the vegetables and thyme and bring back to the boil Simmer for 35 minutes, until reduced to about 1.2 litres/2 pints. Strain once more. The stock is now ready to use or store.

MAYONNAISE

2 egg yolks
2 teaspoons white wine vinegar
½ teaspoon salt
300 ml/10 fl oz olive oil

Before you start, make sure all the ingredients are at room temperature. Put the egg yolks, vinegar and salt into a mixing bowl; place the bowl on a tea towel, to stop it slipping around. Using a wire whisk, gradually beat the oil into the egg mixture, a little at a time, until you have incorporated it all.

The Seafood Restaurant
Riverside
Padstow
Cornwall PL28 8BY
Tel: 01841 532 700
Fax: 01841 532 942
Email: reservations@rickstein.com

Padstow Seafood School
Riverside
Padstow
Cornwall PL28 8BY
Tel: 01841 532 700
Fax: 01841 533 344
Email: seafoodschool@rickstein.com

St Petroc's Hotel & Bistro
4 New Street
Padstow
Cornwall PL28 8EA
Tel: 01841 532 700
Fax: 01841 532 942
Email: reservations@rickstein.com

Rick Stein's Cafe
10 Middle Street
Padstow
Cornwall PL28 8AP
Tel: 01841 532 700
Fax: 01841 532 942
Email: reservations@rickstein.com

Stein's Seafood Delicatessen
Riverside
Padstow
Cornwall PL28 8BY
Tel: 01841 532 700
Fax: 01841 532 942
Email: deli@rickstein.com

Stein's
8 Middle Street
Padstow
Cornwall PL28 8AP
Tel: 01841 532 221
Fax: 01841 533 566
Email: steins@rickstein.com

ADDRESSES

This edition first published in the United Kingdom in 2001
by Cassell & Co, a division of the Orion Publishing Group.
Reprinted in 2003 by Weidenfeld & Nicolson, Wellington House,
125 Strand, London WC2R 0BB.
First published in the United Kingdom in 1996 by Weidenfeld & Nicolson

Front cover photograph by Simon Wheeler
Photograph of Rick Stein on page 2 by Peter Rogers
Photograph of Rick Stein on back cover and pages 10-11 by Craig Easton

A CIP catalogue record for this book is available from the British Library

ISBN 0 304 36133 X

Design director David Rowley
Editorial director Susan Haynes
Designed by Clive Hayball
Jacket Typeset in Spectrum MT and Helvetica Neue
Printed and bound in Italy

Weidenfeld & Nicolson
The Orion Publishing Group
Wellington House
125 Strand
London WC2R 0BB